HUBER TH]

A Story of Tuberculosis

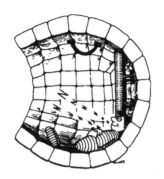

WRITTEN AND ILLUSTRATED BY

HARRY A. WILMER, B.S., M.S., M.D., Ph.D. in Path.

The University of Minnesota Medical School,
Minneapolis

INTRODUCTION BY

J. ARTHUR MYERS, Ph.D., M.D.

Published by the

NATIONAL TUBERCULOSIS ASSOCIATION

1790 BROADWAY, NEW YORK, N Y.

Any resemblance to tubercle bacilli living or dead is purely coincidental; the events portrayed, however, are occurring every day.

First Edition, September 1942

Second Edition, September 1943

Second Printing, 1944

Third Printing, 1946

Fourth Printing, 1949

DEDICATED TO THE MEMORY
OF MY FATHER WHO ALWAYS
WAS AND ALWAYS SHALL BE
MY GREATEST INSPIRATION

INTRODUCTION

In 1941 Dr. Harry Wilmer asked me to read the rough draft of a manuscript entitled "Huber the Tuber." Having known Dr. Wilmer as both medical student and physician and having read other manuscripts by him, I anticipated a work of originality. It was clear to me after reading the manuscript and studying the illustrations, which the author himself had drawn, that here was an ingenious method of telling the story of tuberculosis. It is an entirely new approach in the campaign against tuberculosis, written by one who has himself made a successful recovery from the disease and can therefore approach it sympathetically from the standpoint of both the patient and the physician.

The method of approach in this manuscript is so new and so entirely different that even publishers were at first skeptical. Indeed, it was only through the understanding and vision of tuberculosis control possessed by persons in the office of the National Tuberculosis Association that the manuscript was first made available in book form in 1942. Enthusiastic reviews by lay and medical editors appeared in magazines and journals. The demand for the book far exceeded the anticipation of its supporters. Soon people in all walks of life and of all ages were reading "Huber the Tuber," and while they were being entertained, they were also receiving valuable information. This book has proved of value in health education among employers and employees in industry, among military groups, and among others actively engaged in public health. It has been thoroughly tested and found to be an effective weapon. Dr. Wilmer tells the story in a way that everyone can understand and in such an authentic manner that his book should find a place in every household in America. Here is another example of the innumerable services rendered by the National Tuberculosis Association which merits the support of every citizen.

J. ARTHUR MYERS
Professor of Preventive Medicine and
Public Health, University of Minnesota

September 1944

WANTED

HUBER THE TUBER

Huber the tuber caused a higgledy -
pigglety--thinggumabob —
To be eaten in the attic of the
pugeldy lungle-de-lug —
He is acidy fastidy conserlative chug-
And is dangerous to the pulomatry
and the ker-chuggety-slug.

Corpusle & Catchum

PREFACE

America has a great record in its fight against tuberculosis. The death rate per 100,000 has been reduced from 194 in 1900 to 33.5 in 1947. To insure that tuberculosis is held within bounds, everyone should know the simple facts about this disease, for knowledge does much to prevent and to cure it.

Who gets tuberculosis?

Anybody. Tuberculosis respects no one: doctor, lawyer, merchant, chief. But it is essentially a disease reflecting poor living conditions, often a disease of poverty, of people whose general resistance is low. When one individual of a family living under unhealthy and crowded conditions contracts the disease, the ideal circumstances exist for its spread from one to another, just like any infectious disease. But even among the rich with spacious homes and good foods, tuberculosis may spread through the entire family if one member who is sick and does not know it sows the germs. While tuberculosis causes more deaths than any other disease between the ages of 15 and 34, still, it can develop at any age so that now it constitutes one of the problems involved in the care of old people.

How is tuberculosis spread?

Tuberculosis is not inherited. Only the tubercle bacillus can cause tuberculosis. The germs fly on droplets of moisture or pulverized dust and are inhaled into the lungs. In this way these dangerous germs are passed from a person with active tuberculosis to a person who does not have it.

The most important contacts are household and industrial contacts where the person spreading the germs is in intimate association with those about him. One member of a family may infect every other member, and one sick worker may soon have spread tuberculosis to those about him.

There is also a possibility of contracting this disease from accidental contacts, such as the man who sits next to you on the street car or bus and coughs, the man who spits in the street, or the girl who sneezes or "talks droplets" in your face.

A less common method of transmitting tuberculosis occurs when children play on the floor or sidewalk, soil their hands or playthings and carry the germs from their hands to their mouths. Tubercle bacilli may be left on a spoon, drinking cup, whistle, pencil, or pipe—and the next person who puts these articles in his mouth gives the germs a chance to get inside his body. A tuberculous mother who kisses her baby is almost sure to plant some of her germs in her child. And likewise, servants, relatives, or members of a household who have tuberculosis—and do not know it—may infect a tiny child.

How can we keep from getting tuberculosis?

There is no sure way, but the best protection is to follow simple and sensible health rules: get plenty of rest and sleep; eat sufficient nourishing foods; avoid overwork for long periods of time; spend some time in the out-of-doors, the sunshine, and the fresh air; cover your nose and mouth whenever you sneeze or cough and see that others do the same; avoid excesses.

What are the symptoms of tuberculosis?

While the symptoms of tuberculosis are important, and everyone should know them, still, early cases of tuberculosis present very few, and sometimes no symptoms. Apparently well people may have tuberculosis, and for this reason periodic X-ray examinations and routine X-ray surveys of groups of people may reveal the disease before there are any symptoms. Unless tuberculosis is looked for in this way, the disease may be rather far advanced before symptoms have developed far enough to cause the patient to consult a physician.

Assuming by now you have dispelled any silly notion that "it can't happen to you," the most important thing is to be alert for the first signs and symptoms which might occur. Everybody knows that the earlier you treat a disease the better the chances are for recovery, and TB is no exception. Unfortunately, it is a sneak disease creeping upon its victim, striking swiftly, striking softly. The early warnings which tuberculosis give are few, and even as these few symptoms progress they might easily be disregarded unless you know and respect them:

1. Fatigue
2. Loss of energy
3. Indigestion
4. A persistent cough

These are the four earliest warnings and they must be recognized because the germs are playing for keeps. If you neglect the first signs, the disease will progress and the warnings finally become so obvious that they cannot be ignored. The fatigue or tiredness will grow into exhaustion; the loss of energy is replaced by fever and sweating; the indigestion leads to progressive loss of weight; the cough which was dismissed as a "cigarette cough" or a "hang-over" from a cold or the grippe becomes a body-shaking cough and sputum is raised from deep in the chest.

Less often tuberculosis strikes suddenly with serious warnings. There may be a hemorrhage from the lung, possibly just a tiny streaking of blood in the sputum. Occasionally the first symptom is a sharp pain in the chest—pleurisy—which must never be passed over lightly.

How is tuberculosis diagnosed?

Upon the least suspicion competent medical advice must be sought. Occasionally the doctor can diagnose tuberculosis by listening to your chest with his stethoscope, but as a rule the diagnosis is made or excluded by the chest X-ray picture. The diagnosis is, therefore, made by the X-ray and by finding tubercle bacilli in the sputum.

A simple test—the tuberculin, or Mantoux test—in which a small injection is made into the forearm, if positive, means you have been infected. It does not tell whether or not you have active tuberculosis. Only the X-ray picture can decide. Everyone with a positive Mantoux test should have a chest X-ray picture every year!

What is the treatment of tuberculosis?

Tuberculosis is curable. Rest is the treatment. This means rest in the medical sense—not just change of scene or work—but absolute rest flat in bed 24 hours a day. Next in importance, granted of course that you have competent medical care, is a balanced diet including milk, meat, eggs, fruits, and vegetables. Although fresh air is necessary, it is not wise to freeze or broil. Climate is not as important as was once thought. Careful study of different sanatoriums shows that the treatment of tuberculosis is successful in any climate in the United States.

The best place to "take the cure" is at a sanatorium, where everything has been planned with that one purpose in mind. Rest is enforced, diets are nutritious, medical and surgical care is readily available, and everyone is concentrating on the one problem of getting well.

In addition to rest in bed, it is sometimes advisable to increase the rest of the diseased lung by putting a pocket of air in the space between the chest wall and the lung. This collapses or pushes down the lung and is called "pneumothorax." There are also other procedures for collapsing the lung. Only a competent physician can determine what type of treatment is needed in any individual case. Streptomycin now supplements medical and surgical care.

What happens to the germs when they get into the lung?

Many things can happen. In the first place, they are met by the body cells whose job it is to fight the tubercle bacilli—the foreigners. The outcome depends somewhat upon the size virulence of the invading forces, and upon the strength of the resisting forces. Often a quick decision one way or the other is reached. Since almost everyone inhales tubercle bacilli sometime, and relatively few people develop tuberculosis, it is obvious that the tubercle bacilli are usually defeated. That is another way of saying that there is an important difference between being infected and having the disease.

The tough body cells encircle the tubercle bacilli and prevent them from spreading destruction. In a sense they rope off a danger zone. Eventually calcium (lime) is deposited in a hard, stony little shell around the invading germs. At this point the germs are trapped, and they "go to sleep" waiting for an opportunity to escape and cause tuberculosis when the body resistance is low or is caught off guard. What happens after that is the story which follows

HUBER THE TUBER tells what might happen in one instance when tubercle bacilli are inhaled and cause tuberculosis. It does not pretend to tell the whole story of tuberculosis, but it does highlight important facts well worth remembering.

On each page facing an illustration, is a short whimsical narrative telling about Huber's adventures. At the bottom of each of these pages is a short medical description interpreting the story and drawings in the light of scientific facts It is suggested that you read through the story following the narrative consecutively, and when you are finished, turn back and read the medical story.

Acknowledgment: I am indebted to Doctor Merriam Fredricks and to Mr. Frederick Feikema for their help in conceiving the original story of Huber, and also to Mr. Roger E. Joseph, Mr. Irvin K. Nelson, Miss Kathleen Ann Wurm, and Mr. S. M. Sharpe for their help and encouragement I am grateful to the National Tuberculosis Association for its kindness and understanding. But most important I am immeasurably indebted to Doctor Harry E. Kleinschmidt, formerly Director of Health Education of the National Tuberculosis Association, now a Medical Director of the American Red Cross, for his indispensable advice and criticism.

H. A. W.

LIST OF CHARACTERS IN THE DRAMA*

Villains:

HUBER THE TUBER...Conservative Villain

BOVY...Huber's Sweetheart

NASTY VON SPUTUM..Arch-Villain

    NASTY'S COHORTS:

        Rusty the Bloodyvitch

        Huey the Long Tuber

        Gobbles

        Gorring

        Tojotuber

Heroes:

CORPUSCLE LIPSKY..Chief of Home Guard

    ENTIRE HOME GUARD ARMY:

        Signal Corps

        Military Police

        Mechanized Forces

        Infantry

        Engineer Corps

        Giant Cell

*Tubercle bacilli are all villains, even though some are more virulent or dangerous than others. The conservative villain, Huber the Tuber, is an example of the less virulent form, while the arch-villain Nasty von Sputum and his cohorts are the most virulent forms. Both kinds enter our body and they get all mixed up. None of them are innocuous. *Home Guard* cells are the army which fights the invading enemy—the germs. This army is made up of white blood cells and a special type of Body Cell produced in the host to fight the tubercle bacilli. The Home Guard Army is organized just like any first rate modern army, complete with service and supply, infantry and commandos, mechanized forces and general staff.

HUBER THE TUBER, Nasty von Sputum, Rusty the Bloodyvitch Huey the Long Tuber, and their friends left their old home. was a hurried departure and quite involuntary. But they wer carried away in the breath of a moment; during a cough they left o some droplets of moisture.

Every new case of tuberculosis comes from an old case of tuberculosis! It is spread from one person to another by tubercle bacilli carried in droplets of moisture flying from the mouth and nose during coughing, sneezing, and talking

They were inhaled by an unsuspecting host. Huber, large for his age and always a leader slid down the windpipe first. Suddenly he bumped his bottom on the bottom. He sat scratching his head, puzzled over which of two branch-line airways to explore, when all at once the Tubers were swept into the left airway by a deep breath.

About 13,000 people between 15 and 34 years of age die annually in the United States from tuberculosis It is the leading cause of death from disease in this age group. Tubercle bacilli are the enemy of mankind. It causes the most widespread of human infections and therefore everyone should know the story of tuberculosis

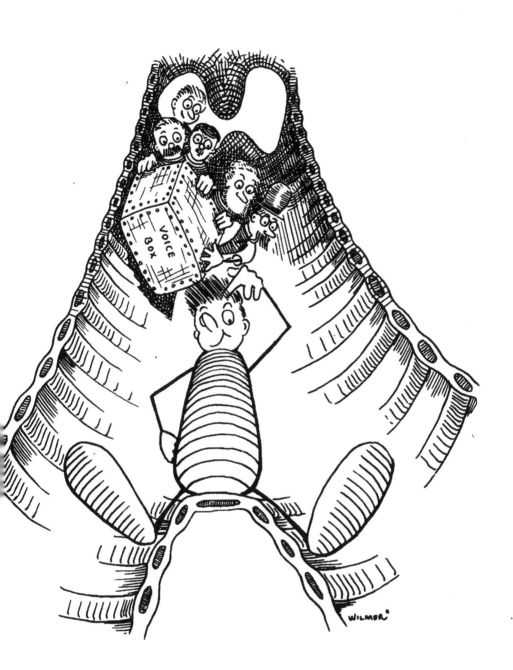

Huber and his friends, who like all Tubers are hard to shake, g[e]
jammed into an airsac. This was Lungland, but all the Tubers were [s]
crowded that something had to be done. The zoning laws had nev[e]
taken account of Tubers, and living room was not provided for ther[n.]

Nasty von Sputum, a virulent Tuber, started slashing his swo[rd]
around and shouting, "give me air," as he cut into another airsac. Rus[s]
the Bloodyvitch wanted to throw his bomb up in the lung attic to mal[e]
a cavity big enough to move around in. Huey the Long Tuber paced u[p]
and down on Huber's stomach screeching at the top of his lungs, "Eve[ry]
Tuber a King! Build your castles in the airsacs! Eat your way to posterity[!"]

Tubercle bacilli that are inhaled come to lodge in the airsacs of the lung. Some tuberc[le]
bacilli are apparently more virulent than others. Whenever tubercle bacilli enter the bo[dy]
they are dangerous. The great majority of people have inhaled tubercle bacilli at one tim[e]
or other.

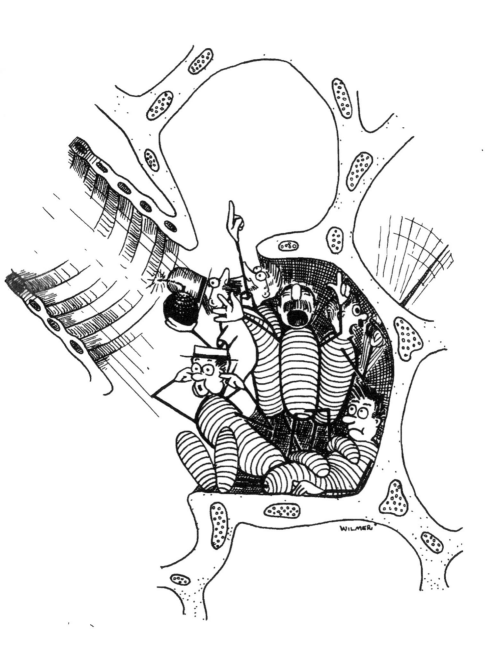

Huber, a conservative of the mild strain, stood up and shouted, "An airsac for everyone!" This simple solution had never occurred to the other Tubers. They, of course, were stupid compared to Huber.

All the screeching Tubers had been unaware that they had attracted the other inhabitants of Lungland. For that matter Huber was the only one who gave any thought to the fact that their noisy discussion might irritate the original occupants of Lungland, who naturally had high priority rating and objected to any intruder.

The Signal Corpsmen, mercenary white blood cell soldiers hired by the Home Guard Army, detected the Tubers. Not knowing the nationality of the invaders, they broadcast the word the length and breadth of Lungland, *"Foreign bodies!"*

The immediate response of the body to the first invasion of the tubercle bacilli is the dispatch of white blood cells to the site of infection.

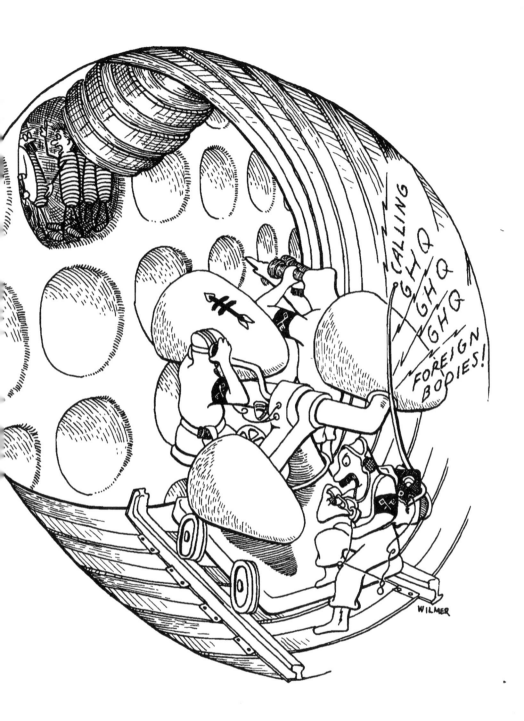

After Huber had won the attention of all the Tubers he told them, "Don't blow a cavity; don't cut the lung up. Everyone can have an airsac to himself. Chew slowly, enjoy yourself, and eat yourself out a house and home! If you start a lot of trouble you will meet the Home Guard Army. Beware of Corpuscle Lipsky, the Chief of the Home Guard. So, my friends, if we build homes of calcium stones all will be well. We do not want a big spread; we do not want miliary-military aggression—we want peace and quiescence."

Huber had won them all over. He was elected Chief Goohn of Tuberville I (Tuber talk for mayor of the town). They all started working, and soon the Tubers settled down in the calcified section.

The initial site of infection usually becomes calcified due to the deposition of calcium from the blood stream. This can be seen on the X-ray as a tiny white spot.

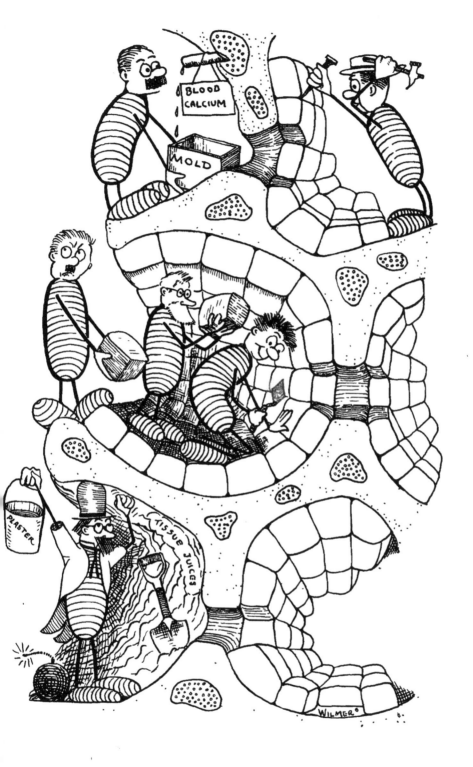

Huber, whose spotless home life endeared him to the conservative voters, had a copy of "The Magic Mountain" and settled down on his doorstep to read it. Soon he fell asleep and slept for twenty tuberculears!

Once the tubercle bacilli are walled in by calcium they usually remain inactive and cause no trouble. However, we can think of them as sleeping or "playing possum" because under circumstances favorable to the bacilli they may escape and cause the greatest harm.

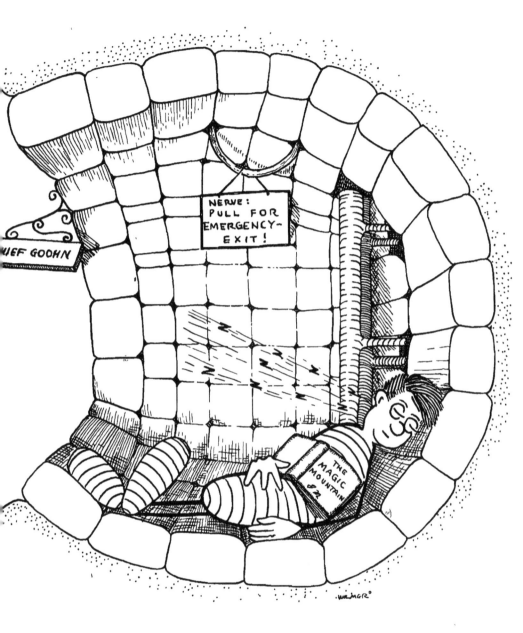

But while he slept all was not well in Tuberville. Having caught their Chief Goohn napping, the Virulents got together to plan a new order for Lungland. Nasty von Sputum was all for a military spread and the sooner the better. He was not satisfied with quiescence. This peace was driving him wild. He told them of his special plans for a big spread —a miliary-military affair.

Rusty the Bloodyvitch was all for throwing his bomb, but the others persuaded him to wait for more explosive times and to first bore from within. Before they could do anything they had to get rid of Huber because he was a conservative. With Huber out of the way they could infiltrate all over lungland.

Thus they plotted and planned while Huber slept. If they could only get rid of the Chief Goohn!

The factors which aid the tubercle bacilli (predisposing factors) are: a lowering of general body resistance, deficient nutrition, exposure to cold and wet due to insufficient clothing, poor living conditions such as too many people in small rooms, deficient ventilation, irregular living, alcoholism, and other excesses.

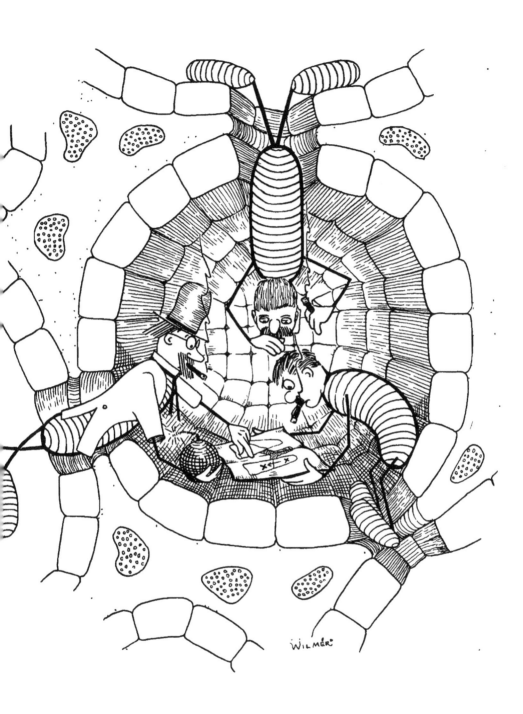

The opportunity that Nasty, Rusty and Huey had been waiting for came at last. Their host went on a drinking spree, staying out all hours of the night and smoking incessantly. Because Huber lived on the corner of Bronchus and Main, the smoke was inhaled past him first, and he awoke on the verge of suffocation.

Nasty von Sputum brought Huber a glass of fresh, cold tissue juice to drink and told him it would stop his cough. But the soft drink was spiked with blood alcohol tapped from their drunk host, and Huber, who usually drank only socially, passed out. Rusty the Bloodyvitch propped him up by the airway and Huey the Long Tuber pulled the nerve marked use for emergency exit only. This caused the Host to cough, and poor Huber was blown up the airway.

The radicals congratulated themselves. The *coup d'ètat* had been a success!

If we allow our health to run down we give the tubercle bacilli the opportunity that they seem to wait so patiently for. They may wait in the lungs quietly for years and years. Don't be an ally of this germ! When active tuberculosis develops there is some point at which the scales just tip in favor of the bacilli.

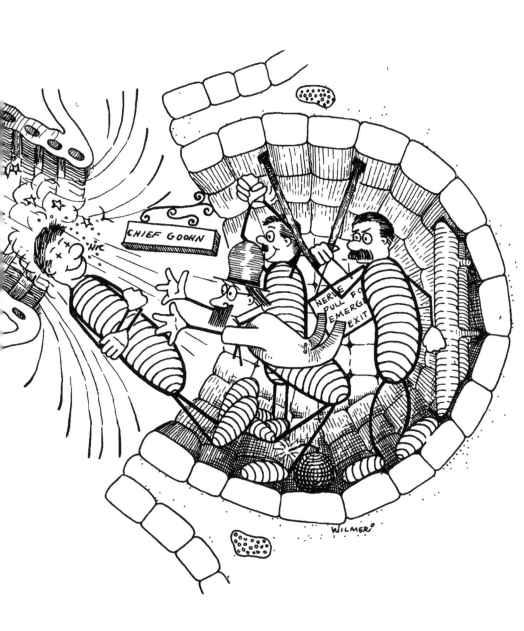

When Huber woke up he had a terrible hangover. After a struggle to keep both eyes open at once, he found himself sitting at the bottom of the windpipe again. "This is where I came in," he said, and started to stand up, but his legs were as weak as his memory of the night before. Huber was almost in tears when suddenly a pretty little girl Tuber coasted demurely down the windpipe to his side.

She did not look like any girl he had known, but he slid over next to her and boldly asked, "What's your name?"

"I'm Miss Bovine Bug," she said, "but my friends call me 'Bovy.' I'm only a country Tuber girl. My home was Udderville, but I took a milk train out and came here in a glass of milk. I'm really an ignorant miss, but I love you!"

If Huber's mind was a blank since last night, Bovy's mind was a blank since birth. He asked her to marry him because he had finished reading "The Magic Mountain."

Tubercle bacilli are slender rod shaped living organisms. Of the types which cause human disease the human and bovine strains are most important. The latter is found in unpasteurized milk from tuberculous cows. Through tremendous efforts bovine tuberculosis has been practically eradicated in the United States. Dr J. Arthur Myers has called this "man's greatest victory over tuberculosis!"

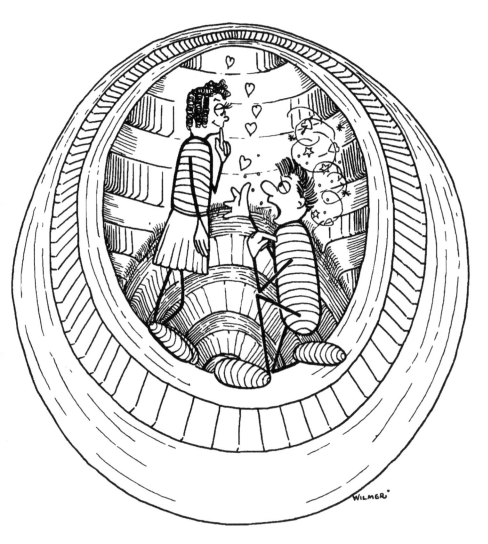

They honeymooned traveling down the Tuberville Trolley to the end of the big airway. When they came to Tuberville I, everything had been changed. There was a border guard behind a barricade of lymph nodes.

"What's the meaning of this?" blustered Huber, who knew all the time that trouble had started.

"You can't enter Tuberville. There is a battle going on inside. I'm Corpuscle Nelson of the Body Immune Forces, with strict orders to keep all snooping Tubers out. Scat! Scram!"

Huber became huffy and told the guard that he was Chief Goohn of Tuberville, but this just made Corpuscle Nelson laugh loud and long. "We know what you Tubers have been doing all the time. The Signal Corps had you spotted the moment you first invaded. The Immune Forces have all of Lungland under guard."

Huber, who had been schooled in diplomacy as well as politics, tried a new approach. "Oh, Corpuscle Nelson," he said, "I know you are doing your duty as you see it, and I have always admired you. You are so handsome and strong. I'm only a conservative Tuber, and Bovy and I are on our honeymoon. Won't you help us?"

This did the trick, and the guard in a moment of weakness confided to Huber that up in the very top of Lungland the Immune Forces were not yet on guard. This, Corpuscle Nelson said, he had on the best authority.

Don't ever think that you are only a spectator in the tuberculosis campaign. The early symptoms are: cough, weakness, loss of weight, raising of sputum, night sweats, fever in the afternoon, or any combination of these—and sometimes others. Delay in consulting your doctor only courts disaster.

Huber was never one to question authority. He lead Bovy to a airway and they were inhaled to the very top of Lungland.

But Huber's past life in Tuberville reared its ugly head—in fact tw heads. These were spies called Gobbles and Gorrings, and were sent b Nasty von Sputum.

While Bovy and Huber were making love, Gobbles and Gorrin went about their sinister business. The plans for the new order called fe a big cavity and Gobbles gobbled and Gorring gored. Thus they ate big cavity and would have made it bigger had not Huber suddenly looke up and seen them. The spies quickly jumped down the small airwa head first.

The development of active tuberculosis leads to a consolidated area in the lung. If the does not scar quickly, a cavity may form. This cavity is made when the necrotic or dea center of a diseased area is drained off and coughed up. The cavity is therefore like an abscess whose walls prevent a general blood stream infection. The cavity is proof tha the body possesses strong resisting powers. The tubercle bacilli do not, of course, actuall eat holes in the lungs.

But the damage was already done. Huber wanted to build this cavity into a mansion lined with calcium stones but all Bovy wanted to do was make goo-goo eyes. They compromised and made goo-goo eyes. Married life in an attic wasn't all it was supposed to be and Huber soon realized that his young helpmate wasn't ready to settle down.

Bovy discovered that the Blood Stream ran right under their living room. Without a worry that the living room might settle, she remembered all the fun she had had swimming in the lovely clean streams at Udderville. Bovy told Huber she wanted to go wading, but Huber said that he would have none of such nonsense. The current is so fast, he told her, that she would not be able to resist the capillary attraction.

One day while Huber slept—things always happened while he slept—she ate a small piece of lung so she could go wading in the Blood Stream.

In the acute miliary or generalized form of tuberculosis the disease completely overwhelms the forces of resistance and the tubercle bacilli are spread by the blood stream to every organ in the body. This very rare form is rapidly fatal.

Huber had been right. He always was. No sooner had she put her big toe in, than her head followed! There was an awfully loud "SLURRP," and it woke Huber up. Already fluid was gushing in from the swimming hole Bovy had dug in the floor.

The tuberculous portion of the lung erodes into a blood vessel when there is a hemorrhage. Most instances of hemorrhage are merely streaking of blood in the sputum due to the erosion of tiny vessels.

"Help!" Huber cried. The fluid level was rapidly rising. But he had read other books besides "The Magic Mountain" and remembered the story of the little Dutch boy who stopped the leak in the dike with his finger. Huber held his finger in the leak until all the fluid had drained out.

The neighbors below didn't complain about the dripping fluid, but worked on the host (he was not a landlord since Tubers don't pay rent) until he coughed it all up.

In some cases there will be large hemorrhage when a large vessel is eroded. This is, indeed, a frightening occurrence although usually not dangerous. There are other causes of the expectoration of blood than tuberculosis

While Huber was fretting, very lonesome without his Bovy, she was awash in the Blood Stream. Finally she was washed ashore at a Southern city called "Synovia." This was in a foreign country very different from Lungland located at a small isthmus between those strange tropical countries of Femoria and Tibia.

Bovy did not know the ways of a big city and she ended up in a joint. Everyone drank so much joint fluid that the whole joint got stiff.

And there Bovy still languishes, separated from the man she loves, a horrible example of what happens to adventurous wives, even in Lungland.

Bovine tubercle bacilli may cause crippling bone and joint disease. In almost every country except the United States bovine tuberculosis in its many forms is common. One should show extreme caution in exposing children to unpasteurized milk.

Huber couldn't shake memories of Bovy in the old cavity and tried to develop some outside interests. He collected some tubes and built a radio set. When he turned it on there was startling news: "Testing, testing," the announcer called. "Mantoux testing, One, Two, Three; Testing, Testing! That is all."

This meant trouble. The host must have become worried when all that fluid came up and gone to see a doctor. Huber was right (naturally). The doctor had applied a Mantoux test, which was positive. All Tubers are allergic to that horrible word: *Mantoux!*

The Mantoux test determines whether the patient is sensitive (allergic) to minute amounts of tuberculin which is injected into the skin of the forearm. It is an extremely accurate test to tell whether the patient has ever been infected with tubercle bacilli. While the great majority of people have been infected, naturally very few people are sick with the disease. This distinction between infection and disease is most important and for a definite answer we turn to the X-ray picture. Every person with a positive Mantoux test should have an X-ray picture of his lungs every year!

An x-ray picture was taken. Huber would have objected, but he wasn't consulted. He was hopping mad because he couldn't get life insurance anymore. (No Tuber Life Insurance Company will issue a policy after an x-ray picture has been taken.)

Even though Huber was a little out of focus, the picture showed a terrible mess in Lungland. In the middle of the·cavity Huber stood scratching his head and mumbling under his breath, "doctors are . . . (censored) * . . ."

---

* All statements deleted were thought unfit for popular consumption

On the basis of the X-ray picture and the clinical story the diagnosis of tuberculosis is made. A "spot" or shadow usually first appears in the upper lobes of the lungs. This "spot" later may become a cavity seen as a "hole" in the lung. The doctor can follow the disease by X-ray pictures through all its stages to healing and thereby regulate the patient's treatment. It goes without saying that the microscopic tubercle bacilli cannot be seen on the X-ray picture.

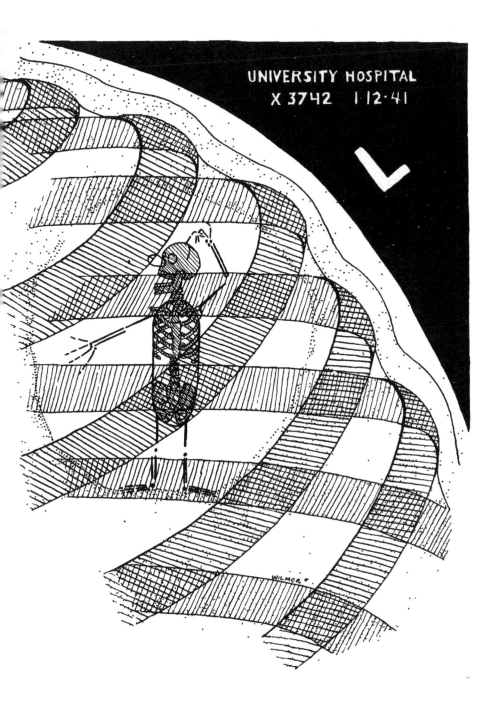

The host was ordered to bed immediately. This was bad news for all the Tubers because it gave the Home Guard the chance to completely mobilize. A warrant for Huber's arrest was issued. Similar warrants were issued for each Tuber. As soon as Corpuscle Lipsky heard that the host was in bed he summoned the Commanding Corpuscle of each branch of the Army. The only Sergeant in the Home Guard was murdered years ago, and since that time the highest rank has been Corpuscle.

The branches of the Army are: Signal Corps, to locate the Tubers; Military Police, to arrive at the scene of trouble first (also hired white cell soldiers); Infantry, to destroy the Tubers; Mechanized forces to bolster resistance (antibodies and immune bodies); and Engineer Corps which ensnare the fleeing Tubers in barbed wire and imprison them in calcium jails.

As soon as tuberculosis is diagnosed the patient is put to bed. Rest alone frequently suffices to heal tuberculosis The best place to take the "cure" is in a sanatorium because of its regulated life, proper foods, fresh air, and because they are staffed with competent experts in the field of tuberculosis. Rest allows the body to fight under the best conditions. In a sense it permits the body forces to concentrate on one thing—on tuberculosis. The tubercle bacilli that are in the lung are first met by the highly mobile white blood cells, and finally by the special cells called "monocytes" which are apparently best able to cope with the tubercle bacilli

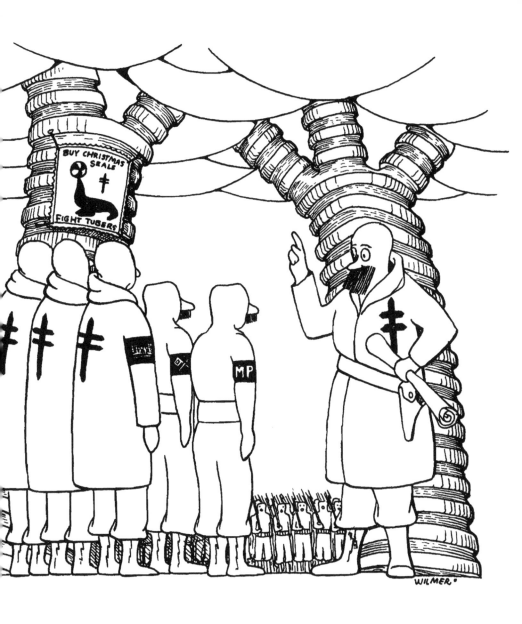

The Military Police (MP) carrying guns and bayonets trapped Huber in his attic hole. The cavity was so big that they could not quite reach him with their bayonets, but poor Huber could not move. In this way they threatened the fugitive with starvation. "I'm surrounded!" Huber cried.

That evening a terrific wind began to blow. The longer the wind blew the more the attic shook, and gradually the walls and ceiling moved closer to him. Just as Huber was trying to make his whole life flash before his eyes as it is supposed to do, the wind quieted down and things stopped closing in on him.

Nature in the vast majority of cases heals the disease and there is a tendency to recover with any proper method of treatment, and sometimes with none. One of the purpose of medical and surgical treatment is to produce more recoveries than would ordinarily be anticipated. Tuberculosis is a chronic disease reckoned in months and years and not day and weeks. There are no clock watchers with tuberculosis—there are only calendar watchers!

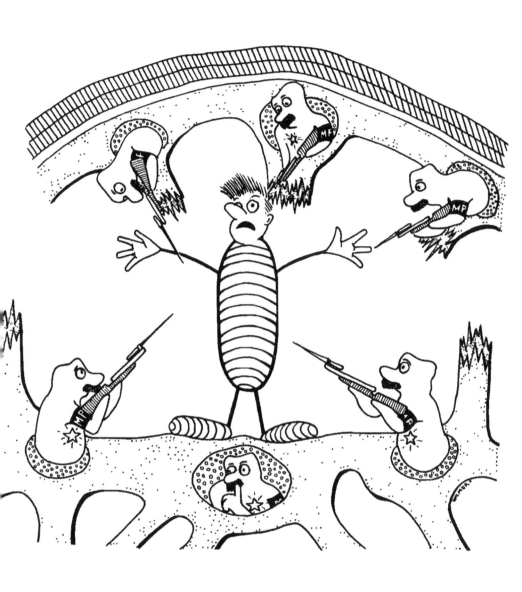

Huber was very smart, and he knew that the doctor had put a needle in the chest wall and was pushing air in the space around the lung. This type of wind storm is like a cyclone in Lungland. Huber had once heard a doctor call it a "pneumothorax," but he knew it was really an inflation, brought on following a period of unrest.

He was just about pinned in by the Military Police. If the ceiling or walls came any closer he would suffocate. At best he would die from want of something to eat; at worst the antibodies might eat him. To be fed or be food, that was the question!

The purpose of bed rest is to rest the entire body. The purpose of "pneumothorax" is to close the cavities and rest the lungs which expand and contract 25,000 times a day throughout life. The pneumothorax consists of injecting air into the pleural cavity—the space between the lungs and the chest wall. A small amount of local anesthesia makes this relatively painless. Normally the lungs fill this pleural space because a vacuum or negative pressure holds it out. But the lung is a rather elastic organ and its normal tendency is to collapse. By putting a pocket of air in this space the lung is partially collapsed or allowed to retract. It is possible to collapse both lungs partially. The air must be replaced at intervals because it is absorbed.

Huber glanced about him, and when the M.P.'s seemed slightly relaxed (no doubt overconfident) he kicked two of them in the teeth, and yelled "FIRE!" This affront took them so much aback that he escaped in a split second by way of an adhesion.

He gasped with relief as he took stock of things to come while sitting on an adhesion in the Great Pleural Canyon.

Pneumo," as pneumothorax is familiarly called, is not indicated in all cases nor is it possible to establish even in all those cases where it is desirable. When and if it should be started is purely and simply a matter for the doctor to decide. The pneumo is like a splint applied to a broken limb to keep the bone immobilized and allow it to heal. It is not as effective as a cast but reduces the frequency and depth of respiration in most cases. The walls of the cavity are forced together Everyone knows that it takes a wound longer to heal if it is kept open. A tiny cut on your knuckle takes longer to heal than a larger cut on your arm. "Pneumo" also retards the spread of bacteria and their toxic products. Thus there is less chance of spreading the disease to unaffected parts of the lungs and the symptoms are relieved

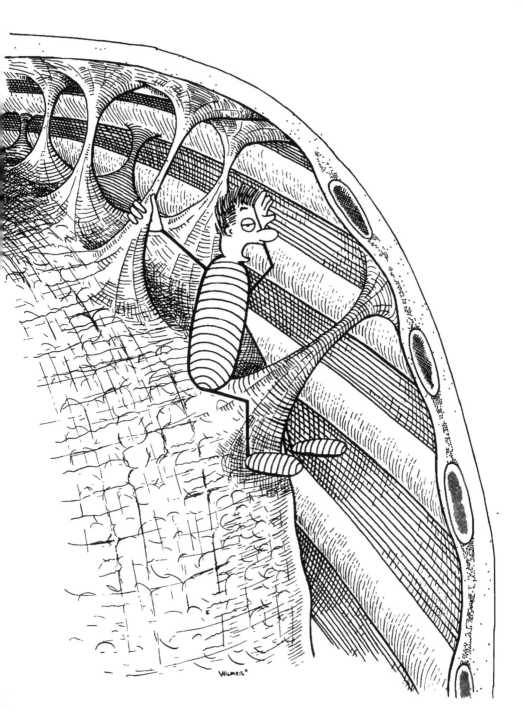

Suddenly a bright light came through the chest wall on the end of periscope. It twisted and turned until it spotted the adhesion that Hube had been sitting on. He jumped back behind some other adhesions an was nearly scared to death when a horrible animal—probably an all gator—came through the chest wall beside the periscope. With red ho teeth he seared the adhesions in two.

When the adhesions interfere with the effective collapse of the lung they may b severed by an operation called "pneumonolysis." Two instruments are manipulated in th pleural space through two tiny incisions in the side between the ribs. The doctor ca actually look at the adhesions through a wonderful optical instrument with a series o lenses and mirrors—the thoracoscope. It has a tiny electric light on the end. He the severs the adhesions with the other instrument—the electrocautery—as he watches it.

When the last adhesion was severed the lung suddenly fell way down. As it receded from the chest wall there came into view a lake at the bottom of the Great Pleural Canyon. "Fluid!" Huber exclaimed as he did a neat swan dive into the water.

Adhesions between the lung and the chest wall will prevent the lung from being collapsed by the "air pocket." Adhesions are formed because the disease in the lung leads to an inflammatory reaction in its covering which is in direct contact with the lining of the chest wall. A scar forms so that they are "glued" together. This interferes with the collapse of the part of the lung which is most important to push down, the diseased area and the cavity. When the adhesions have been cut the lung collapses down farther.

But Huber should have looked before he leaped. Swimming rapidly towards him was a Phagocyte Shark. It was almost upon Huber with its ugly teeth showing when a gurgling sound was heard and the lake went dry.

Occasionally fluid will develop in the pleural space. This is called a "pleural effusion." It is sometimes a complication during the disease, or often the very first indication of tuberculosis. All cases of fluid in the chest are not due to this disease—but most spontaneous cases are tuberculosis. Fluid in the space is diagnosed by the doctor, confirmed by the X-ray, and made certain by the aspiration of a small amount of fluid with a syringe.

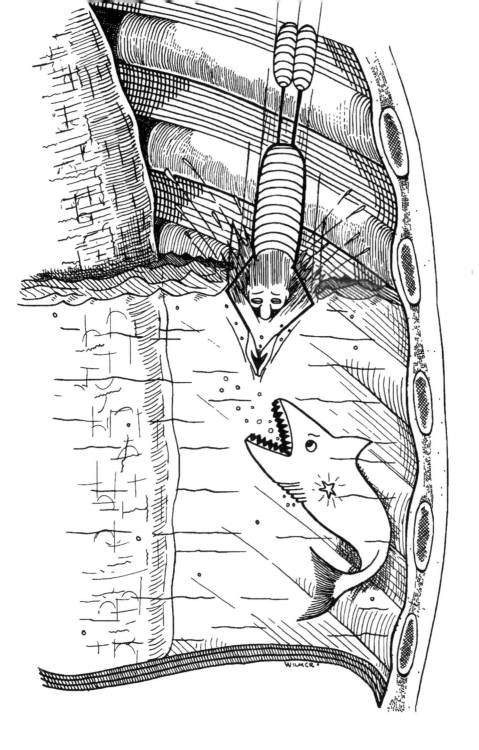

Sticking in the side chest wall at the bottom of the Great Pleura Canyon was a big needle drawing off the fluid. The Tuber-Eating Shark flopped foolishly and Huber hastened to take credit by casually standing on its head and whistling.

But Huber was worried; the lake might be formed again and that would revive the shark. He had to get out of the canyon quick!

If the fluid is not absorbed spontaneously the treatment consists essentially of repeated aspiration and after a while the fluid usually stops being formed The body says, "I make it!" The doctor says, "I take it!" Pretty soon the body gives up. Fluid does not always go away with harmless results; sometimes it becomes infected.

The quickest way out of the canyon was by way of the Lower Lobe "L" (Lymphatic Rapid Transit System). He found the entrance at the side of the lung and after paying his fare opened the valve leading to the "L." Surrounding the entrance were lymph nodes the sight of which was repulsive to Huber. In fact he did not like traveling by the "L" because it was so bumpy; nevertheless it had a sort of irresistible attraction for him.

Tubercle bacilli, just like other germs, are carried by the lymphatic system. This consists of tiny hollow channels, usually accompanying the veins, and like them have valves along the course of the channel or vessel. Interspaced along the course of the lymphatics are lymph nodes. Hundreds of small lymphatic vessels will drain through one lymph node like railroad tracks entering a busy terminal. From the other side of the node fewer vessels emerge from this clearing house and this chain keeps on until there is just one lymphatic vessel entering a big vein near the heart. Thus the lymphatics are a protecting mechanism to prevent invading bacteria from entering the blood system. That is why you have a painful lump under your arm when you have an infection on your hand or arm. This system operates better at rest.

As he came to the end of the trip he heard a lot of shooting and yelling. He had come to the Great Battlefield where Nasty von Sputu and his Tubers were locked in a life and death struggle with the Hom Guard.

The first sight to meet Huber's eyes was a Giant Cell captured the Pancer-Pincers. These were fanatical youngsters led by Tojotube the Field Strategist of the Tubers. He had taught them to pinch-the-pan of the Home Guard since this was their weak spot.

.

The giant cell is a microscopic cell seen in tuberculous diseased tissue. It is quite chara teristic of tuberculosis although found in a few other diseases. It is really a number body cells united in one cell body.

At the extreme rear of the battlefield Nasty von Sputum was in hi bomb-proof, sound-proof dugout directing the war over the T.B.S. (Tu bercle Broadcasting System). A draftsman sat planning a spread to th Promised Land o' Lung. Nasty required all Tubers to salaam in hi great presence.

When doctors say rest is most important in the treatment of tuberculosis they mean both physical and mental rest. The tuberculosis patient has to face certain problems which may result in worry and anxiety. Sometimes they even interfere with his sleeping and eating. The doctor tries to help him overcome these difficulties by sympathetic understanding of the factors which cause them.

Of great importance also is the kindness and understanding which family and friends show. This also applies to those who care for the patient. Visitors and letter writers should not tell patients to "keep a stiff upper lip," "keep smiling," "don't let this get you down" and "don't worry" without actually helping him to do these things. Such advice is easy to give, and may actually be resented. He will get more courage and strength to handle his feelings if he sees his relatives and friends handling theirs. They should show that they are keenly interested in him, helpful and cheerful. Above all don't add your worries to his!

It would be a good idea if family and friends would talk to the patient's doctor or social service workers, if they are available, for advice on this subject. You must help him stay until the doctor thinks he is well enough to leave, so he won't run the risk of being a patient for a second time. But above all remember that the patient is doing his best, and needs encouragement. Let him talk about his illness if he wants to, but don't prod him with questions. You as a visitor *can* be the most important person in the world to him at the time you are with him. You don't have opportunities like that every day.

Tojotuber led the pancer-pincers in a surprise rear attack against a squad of infantry Home Guard advancing up a hill. As soon as the Home Guard jumped and threw up their arms the Tubers would knife them in the back.

Unseen by the pancer-pincers was a Signal Corpsman stationed as a lookout on the top of the hill. Immediately he radioed: "Help! Calling *Mechanized* Forces!"

The battle in the lung is real! The cells of the body actually kill tubercle bacilli, and the tubercle bacilli actually kill the body cells. Here is a struggle between the forces of good and of evil. It truly assumes the proportions of a life and death encounter.

Without a second's delay Corpuscle Lipsky dispatched the mechanized forces: the Immune Bodies and the Antibodies. Under the command of Corpuscle Nelson they raced at breakneck speed to the scene of trouble. It was an easy task for them to rout the pancer-pincers. The infantry then came and killed all the Tubers except Tojotuber. They called the Engineer Corps for him.

Immunity plays an important role in the body struggle against the tubercle bacilli. The exact nature and importance of immunity and allergy are somewhat unsettled so far as scientific research is concerned. Suffice it to say that the marshalling of these forces detrimental to the aggression of the germs. No matter how far advanced the disease is—the body forces will not give up. They will fight to the very end—even though it is losing battle—and who can tell when the scales will be tipped and a losing battle become a winning struggle?

The Engineers captured Tojotuber and immediately surrounded him with barbed wire, which they pulled very, very tight, because some Tubers have been known to escape when it is loose. Corpuscle Lipsky, himself, came to direct the molding of the calcium prison.

The tubercle bacilli are imprisoned in fibrous tissue. While this tissue is being "spun" around the diseased area it is most important that rest be strictly observed. It is like barbed wire, for in an unguarded moment the bacilli may slip through the entanglement and escape. The walled-in area is finally calcified. This is truly a wonderful engineering feat! In a way this battle is like a siege, in the center of which is a no man's land of dead tissue and dead and dying cells. Some of this debris may become liquefied, drained off, and coughed up.

Huber in the meantime had been walking behind the Tuber line and came to a big poster around which was gathered a group of parachute troops. The headlines read: "Nasty von Sputum speaks today unter den Cavity nr. 3: Parachute Troops . . ." It was obvious at once to Huber that these parachute troops were going to be sent out into the world to spread Nasty's mission of destruction. Huber, that conservative, objected to any such barbarian methods.

One cannot learn about tuberculosis by reading newspapers or listening to gossip. You owe it to yourself to know the facts about this disease. The National Tuberculosis Association, your state, county or local tuberculosis association have plenty of accurate, excellent literature which they are eager for you to have. Prejudice and superstition based on ignorance are malignant. Beware of the ignorant who speaks with confidence! The Christmas Seal campaign is the best way that we as individuals can fight tuberculosis. Contribute to it wholeheartedly.

By following the parachute troops, Huber came to "Unter de Cavity nr. 3" which formed a great natural amphitheater. Long banner hung behind the speaker's platform. On them was "S.K." for Spitzkrieg.

A great shout arose as Nasty entered. He began to speak and the audience became deathly silent.

"Parachutists!" he roared (deafening applause). "We are about to shoot you from the special Tuber-Shooting gun! You will leave Lung land, travel up the airways, turn right and go out the windpipe! When you reach the outside pull your parachute cord and float through the air ... A spread for every lung! ...." (deafening applause). *"Go forth and infiltrate!* Eat all the lung you can. Weaken your victim. If there is danger, lay low until the time comes—then strike!" (deafening applause).

After the applause died down everyone left the cavity.

---

* The speech had been carried over the Tubercle Broadcasting System for the benefit of the many shut-in Tubers

Tubercle bacilli may be inhaled on tiny specks of dust which come from tuberculous sputum which has dried and pulverized. The droplets of moisture and the infected dust are like parachute troops suspended in the air and inhaled. Contaminated objects may also spread this disease. Tubercle bacilli in dust which is exposed to the sunlight die very soon.

Once outside, Huber followed the parachute troops. They came to the Special Tuber-Shooting gun and lined up for their turn to be shot up the windpipe.

When the patient knows that he is sick and puts off going to see his doctor he is practically guilty of criminal negligence to himself and society. Avail yourself of the proper care early. *Every new case of tuberculosis comes from an old case of tuberculosis!* This is real preventive medicine whose main stimulus must come from people who do not have tuberculosis . . . or do not YET know they have it. If everyone became interested in this campaign the tubercle bacillus might disappear like the dodo bird

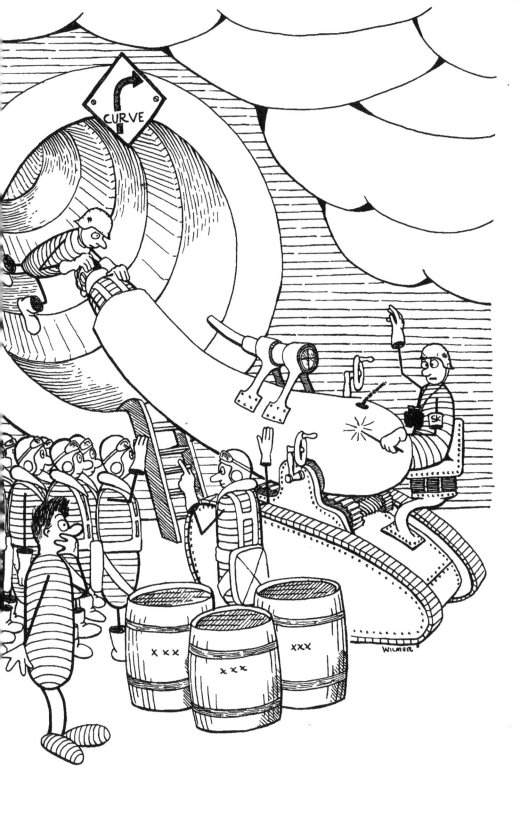

Huber could not hide his rage, and just before the cannon was fire
he jumped up on some powder kegs: "Fellow Tubers!" he cried. "Nas
von Sputum is sending you on a false mission!" The soldiers were :
astonished they simply stood and listened. "Your mission," he continue
"is not to cause trouble in your new homes in distant lands. It is to sett
down and live in comfort. You can even infiltrate a little at first, but liv
in peace and quiescence! And protect your new homes from furth
invasion from without!"

Huber was hastily removed by the secret police.

Any new "cure" when boosted by friends, patients, newspapers or even "well informe
persons, finds the patient in a receptive mood. The "cure," if tried, may even relie
him in a remarkable manner but this is usually psychic and will wear off. If the resul
are not psychic the patient would probably have gotten better anyway. Were this only
question of satisfying a patient's whim it might be excusable . . . but these short cu
to health are a double-edged sword and may find the patients an unfortunate victim
his own hopes!

Huber was brought to Nasty's secret office and asked to explain his treason!

"Treason!" Huber bellowed. "I'm on your side, but you don't know it. You're directing this war all wrong! The Home Guard already has you surrounded. If you had listened to me in the first place this would never have happened."

"So Huber the Tuber is smarter than I am?" Nasty sneered, "How would the great Huber fight this war?"

"In the first place you can only win at such a terrible expense that it won't be worthwhile, for you must completely destroy all of Lungland. Then you will have no place to live. The only hope is for an armistice or a truce based on the status quo!"

"Bah! Truce! That's no fight!" Nasty told him, shaking his finger in Huber's face.

Just then there was the distant rumble of artillery which grew louder and louder until the noise was terrible. Nasty and his aides rushed off to see what was happening, and they locked Huber in the office.

Tuberculosis in all its stages and under most circumstances is curable in a large proportion of cases. Unfortunately there are early cases which have been detected as soon as is humanly possible which have no chance regardless of their care and treatment, but likewise, there are far advanced cases whose chances of survival and recovery are excellent

Crash! Rumble! Crash! BOOM! Huber knew that those sound meant broken ribs—the doctor was taking some ribs out of the host. And that meant a permanent depression would set in. Huber looked out th barred door and saw all the Tubers of Nasty von Sputum's army split up and caught in fibrous bands and adhesions that were forming every where. The Military Police were mopping up the suffering starving Tubers.

When other treatments fail to control the disease an operation is frequently indicate although by no means always. This is called a "thoracoplasty" and parts of the ribs ar removed. The mechanical effect of removing the ribs is the same as the pneumothora The lungs are in a rigid bony cage called the "thorax." By removing parts of the ribs o one side of the chest the unsupported chest wall will cave in, pushing down or collapsin the lung.

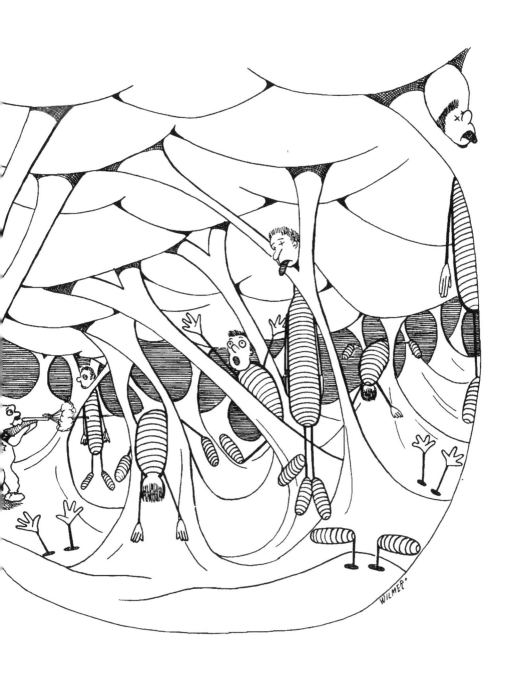

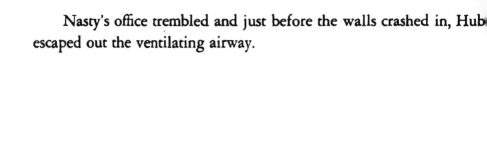

Nasty's office trembled and just before the walls crashed in, Hub escaped out the ventilating airway.

Today streptomycin holds promise for the patient with tuberculosis. The last edition this book in 1946 stated that some day the scientists would find the "magic bullet" t would slay that giant of the earth—tuberculosis. At last we have a faint glimpse of t realization. Actually streptomycin is not, and should not, be used in all cases of tuberculo There are certain dangers involved. It must be given for a long time and all strains tubercle bacilli are not susceptible to the drug. Furthermore new strains—families— tubercle bacilli may grow and be resistant to streptomycin. Let there be no mistake—i is a wonderful advancement in the treatment of tuberculosis It is at the present mom chiefly useful to supplement the ordinary means of treatment. It will never make r less important — rest still remains the tubercle bacilli's Number One Enemy.

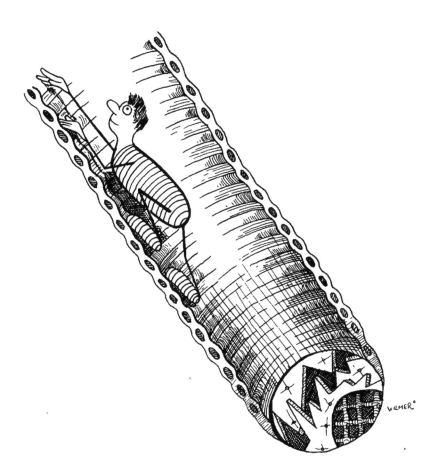

Huber found his way back to his old calcium stone airsac and crawled in. The Depression was catching and crushing the other Tubers and leading to a big victory for the Home Guard Army. But Huber's shelter survived the depression since it was solid stone and unmortgaged. Without a worry about outside affairs, Huber settled down to the ideal life for a conservative Tuber. He slept, and sleeps still.

But Huber is still alive. Maybe a few scattered Tubers of the virulent strain escaped to some other fortified airsacs. They will live imprisoned in calcium because the Home Guard will prevent their escape with barbed wire.

When the patient is discharged from the sanatorium or hospital he has a scar in his lung like a patient has on his abdomen after his appendix is removed. The scarred area may be calcified like a fractured bone which is healed. There must be no more stigma to having the healed tissue in the lung than in the abdomen or in the bone of the leg. There is one important difference: living virulent tubercle bacilli may be found walled in. They may become active again flaring up and causing a recrudescence of the disease. But then every abdominal operation is not a success, nor does every fractured leg cease to cause trouble when taken out of the cast!

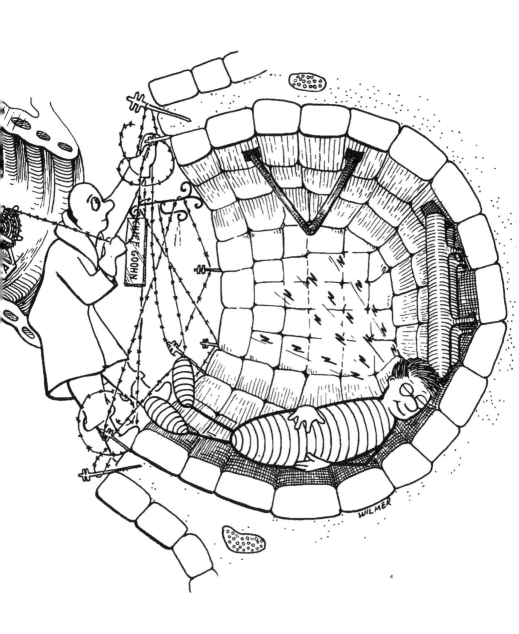

Chief of the Home Guard, Corpuscle Lipsky, summoned all his Army together and there was a great celebration. Bagpipes, with their sqeaks and wheezes, drums with their booming, horns with their "oom pah pah," and trumpets with their clarion calls announced the end of the war!

Corpuscle Lipsky called out: "VICTORY, VICTORY, VICTORY! It is ours! We have defeated the Tubers. Those whom we have not killed are our prisoners of war. So long as we keep them in jail . . . then Lungland is free. LONG LIVE LUNGLAND!"

When the patient has defeated his tubercle bacilli the doctors say that the disease is "arrested" in preference to the word "cured." If the patient remembers *the magic word: moderation,* the arrest of the disease will be permanent. He is well!

MORAL : Don't think it *can't happen to you!*

CPSIA information can be obtained
at www.ICGtesting.com
Printed in the USA
BVHW041402070319
542053BV00012B/202/P